Combating tax evasion –
Possible solutions and
conclusions

By Sebastian Meyer

Digital Edition

Copyright © 2013

Sebastian Meyer

All Rights Reserved

Table of Contents

I. The dimension of tax evasion 1

II. Methods of tax evasion 3

    1.) Founding subsidiaries abroad via real production shift 4

    2.) Introducing transfer pricing on paper 7

    3.) Incurring debts and higher labour costs with hybrid entities on paper 12

III. Conclusion and possible solutions 16

IV. Appendix 21

V. References 32

I. The dimension of tax evasion

Following the consequences of the international financial crisis and the subsequent economic downturn in 2007/08, current news[1] has been determined by discussions and revealing of incentives about exploiting existing regulations and codes because this is subject to evade taxes. During the last years, several secrecy jurisdictions in Europe with a high Financial Secrecy Index (FSI) as shown in Table 1 have announced to loosen their banking secrecy for preventing tax evasion and cooperating with EU and US tax authorities.

Several exemplary studies like (Hebous, 2011), (Buehn et al., 2012) and (Qari, 2012) have already discussed some economic and nonpecuniary motives of non-compliance to national tax laws. They all agree that the action results from the mobility and liquidity of money which is underlined by the hypothesis of Wahl (2005: 14ff.) that"...*the liberalisation of*

---

[1] One example is the recent tax affair of the German Bundesliga Uli Hoeneß: http://www.t-online.de/wirtschaft/id_63345314/uli-hoeness-stellt-strafanzeige-wegen-enthuellung-im-steuer-skandal-.html [Accessed 27 May 2013].

financial markets [...] [gave raise for the global] tax evasion [...]". They conclude that tax evasion are hardly admitted and rather denied. Therefore, delinquents refuse to publicly speak about tax frauds and crimes. Following this first conclusion of tax evasion on the one hand, the head of the Tax Justice Network (TJN) study group Richard Murphy concludes on another that there is no exact quantitative number telling the pure amount of tax evasion. Estimates according to TJN reveal illicit financial flows of US $ 1-1,6 trillion per annum (Henn, 2013). Furthermore, it is also reported that the total global amount of tax evasion is about US $ 28 trillion hidden in around 70 tax havens. (Henn, 2013). Moreover, the annual gains (from interests, dividends, production shifts, etc.) in tax havens amount to approximately US $ 860 billion. (Social Watch Deutschland, 2007).

Based on the quantitative and qualitative dimensions of global tax evasion, this paper analyzes most frequently employed methods of how transnational corporations (TNC) illegally reduce their respective tax liabilities. Eventually, a conclusion is given along with some possible solutions.

II. Methods of tax evasion

The issue of the several ways for TNC's to reduce taxes starts with a brief distinction between tax evasion and avoidance. Tax avoidance includes all activities of a taxpayer resulting in a reduction of the tax payables by legal means. (Sandmo, 2005). To put it differently, a TNC encompasses the transfer of migration of financial and real capital to different jurisdictions or nations for escaping high tax rates. (Quari, 2012). In conclusion, this fact shows a certain overlap between questions of tax avoidance and evasion. The latter is defined as an illegal direct tax optimization because underreporting or not declaring incomes, for instance, is sanctioned with a fine as a consequence. Considering different tax rates abroad also includes, for example, *founding subsidiaries abroad via real production shift, transfer pricing on paper* and *incurring debts and higher labour costs with hybrid entities on paper.* Each presented method firstly starts with a brief description of the organisational setting of the TNC. Thereafter, a qualitative/ quantitative evaluation or a short exemplary case study and conclusion with impact on the decision making process of the TNC follow. Ultimately, a final personal view from an ethical point closes each section.

1.) Founding subsidiaries abroad via real production shift

First and foremost, as depicted in Figure 1, a manufacturing or merchandising TNC is headquartered with its parent company (PC) in the home country (HC) with a higher rate of taxation, like the USA, in comparison to the subsidiary (S) located in a foreign country (FC) with a lower tax rate, like Ireland. After deciding for a cross-national flow of capital like setting up a joint ventures (JV) or engaging in Foreign Direct Investment (FDI), the TNC shifts the main production part, which is the horizontal operating cycle along the value chain (Figure 2), to the lower preferential tax zone in FC. In this example, the FC can also be a tax haven[2] with a high FS-Index[3] as shown in Table 1. Taking the Dublin Dockland area in

---

[2] According to the Organisation for Economic Co-operation and Development (OECD), a tax haven is defined by (almost) no taxes, strict banking secrecy (high FSI), intransparency and no/ little regulation.

[3] We assume a high FS-Index is 50%+.

Ireland as a special tax zone, for example, the S does not only enjoy the fresh air from the North Sea but also has to pay 10% on corporate profits instead of 40% as shown in Figure 3. Putting it in a nutshell, the first crucial incentive includes a positive net tax advantage of 30 % (40% - 10%) between PC and S for the whole holding company as such. Afterwards, for the US, studies proved that a tax decline by only 10% would lead to an increase of the ultimate FDI decision by around 20%. (Ruf, 2007). Consequently, this scenario contradicts the minor role of tax rates for foreign investment decisions (Liebert, 2004). Rather, it complements some determinants of inward FDI like economic potential, business friendliness and quality of life according to Porter (1998) and Zschiedrich (2006) as shown in Table 2. In this context, studies of Ruf (2007) reveal that the elasticity of the foreign investment probability with the incentive to lower tax liabilities is for Ireland 485% in contrast to France of around 50%.

Finally, in my opinion, the production method is mostly determined by lowering the direct tax burden which is a wrong incentive because there is a national tax revenue loss. States cannot tax profits generated abroad because their jurisdiction, residence and business activities are located in the HC. In order to "fair play", the TNC should then set up their new headquarter in the FC (tax haven). Nonetheless, most TNC will refuse doing so as even tax havens with a very strong FS-Index comprising, for instance, Maldives and Nauru, do not fulfil the criteria according to Zschiedrich (2006) to really invest. In sum, they do not play a major role in the international economy. In concordance to Zschiedrich's (2006) investment characteristics abroad, I am also in line with Wachtel's (2009) statement where he points out that *"[... TNC's] located in tax havens are just artificial constructions in order to record transactions that never [externally] happen."* Consequently, the real production shift method gives raise for higher tax competition and lower efficiency of international tax laws. Moreover, it underlines inequality as mostly big TNC make use of it. As any corporation is a nexus of contracts, shown in Figure 4, this method questions sustainability for stakeholders like employees and the state.

However, there is even a smarter option for TNC's to employ legal tricks to further reduce the tax payables by balancing profits and losses until tax liabilities get lesser and lesser.

2.) Introducing transfer pricing on paper

Apart from the real production shift to low-tax countries in tax havens, for instance, the merchandise or manufacturing TNC as shown in Figure 5 can firstly invent ''internally generated prices'' for purchases and sales, also called teaser prices above or below fair market values. (Liebert, 2004). Transfer pricing refers to attempts to attribute a market price to a related party transaction between a PC and S. The organisational setting is alike in the real production shift method.

First of all, the PC, headquartered in HC with high taxation, acquires goods and services from S in FC as shown in Figure 5. The S overprices the goods or services. Remembering the holding structure of a TNC, the uneconomic purchase then reveals as very profitable because the PC in HC with high taxation legally reports higher expenses, due to higher purchase, production and conversion costs, in the income statement and later balance sheet. Subsequently, profits lower in HC whereas those in FC with low taxation are higher. Therefore, S in FC also has a lower tax burden when the PC purchases goods from the S above the market value.

Putting it the other way round also leads to a lower tax burden. (Liebert, 2004). Assuming the same organisational setting, the PC in the HC with high taxation internally sells goods to the S in the FC with low taxation below the fair market value. The PC reports lower revenues, due to a lower sales price below market value. Hence, it ultimately generates a net loss and lowers the tax burden. Referring back to the S in the FC, the latter can re-sell the goods and services with a higher price. The effect is a high profit from the difference between the purchase and sales price for the S in the FC with low taxation. Putting it in a nutshell, PC and S in the holding TNC ''create'' a lower tax burden and higher profit using the transfer pricing method.

In summary, the PC in HC with high taxation purchases/ sells over-/underpriced goods and services abroad. By doing so, it lowers its profit and tax burden. Meanwhile, the S in FC with low taxation purchases/ sells under-/overpriced goods and services.

In doing so, it allows its profits to increase. Finally, the net tax advantage between PC and S is positive.

Shifting from the pure qualitative assessment of the strategy of transfer pricing, a more advanced and numerical example illustrates how any TNC with a PC and S is capable of reducing the tax burden up to 50% of the initial amount. For a better understanding, Wachtel (2009) and Liebert (2004) illustrate an exemplary calculation shown in Figure 6. Calculations show the overall tax burden of 30,5% instead of 38,3% for the PC in the HC with higher taxation. The next step is to ''cook and manipulate the balance accounts''. The TNC Holding internally adds purchase costs of US $ 100,000 to the PC in the HC with higher taxation and sales revenues of US $ 100,000 to the S in the FC with lower taxation. Thus, it reduces the PC's tax liabilities to US $ 0 (initial profit US $ 100,000 – purchase costs US $ 100,000). At the same time, the S in the FC generated a higher profit of US $ 150,000 (initial profit US $ 50,000 + sales revenues US $ 100,000). As shown in Figure 6, the S in FC pays US $ 22,500
on the final profits of US $ 150,000. Subsequently, the overall tax burden is reduced from US $ 45,800 to US

$ 22,500 by around 50%. The tax rate is reduced from 30,5% to 15% on average.

Eventually, from an ethical point of view, transfer pricing with deflated or inflated prices below or above the appropriate value results in hefty tax abuse and losses for the state and society. (Cloer et al., 2008). It creates artificial profits and losses which are internally generated and stored in tax optimisation departments or profit centres (Wahl, 2005). One example is the former Daimler (Chrysler) CEO Jürgen Schrempp who managed to transfer only 0,25% of DaimlerChrysler's global profits to the tax authorities. (Wachtel, 2009). The negative magnitudes of profits shifting and transfer are found in recent studies of Social Watch Deutschland (2006), Klinter et al. (2010), Henn (2013) and Heckmeyer et al. (2008) showing the amounts of transfer pricing in the USA (between US $ 37-53 billion annually), UK (approximately £ 840 million tax break annually) and Germany (between € 60-100 billion corporate tax base gap annually). In my opinion, the real magnitudes are difficult to estimate due to the lack of transparency of TNC's operations, holdings, etc. in tax havens. Furthermore, there are not any exact data for internal swaps within a holding.

Finally, I think the line between legal and illicit practices in transfer pricing is sometimes hard to draw. On the one hand, a real and physical production shift to another country is a good idea, but can quickly turn into wrong incentives if foreign investments are solely determined by tax advantages. On another hand, a fake and paper shift using transfer pricing is a tax fraud and thus the entities concerned have to be sanctioned and fined. Particularly the latter strategy easily gives raise for unreasonable high operating and labour costs whereas the production is comparably very low according to the secondary investigation of Henn (2013). All in all, any TNC should disclose their financial tax information in accordance to fair and faithful characteristics including understandability, relevance, reliability and comparability. In addition to the latter argument, (inter-)national tax authorities along with internal revenue services should keep a closer eye on a transaction where a ''plastic bucket from the USA to Pakistan costs US $ 972'' (Henn, 2013). In doing so, one could possibly reduce illicit flows due to transfer pricing.

Nevertheless, TNC's methods of tax planning and evasion may go beyond the real production shift or the paper transfer pricing.

3.) Incurring debts and higher labour costs with hybrid entities on paper

A further possibility of illegally reducing tax burden and liabilities of the PC in the HC with high taxation is to firstly borrow funds from the S abroad. (Henn, 2013). There exists a legal loan or bond contract with all rights and obligations between the PC and the hybrid entity of the S. In other words, the PC is internally financed with a liability by the hybrid entity. The crucial point is to understand how the hybrid entity of the whole TNC Holding is treated from a tax point of view. As depicted in Figure 7, the tax law in the FC treats a hybrid entity as ''non-transparent'' and thus taxable. Meanwhile, the tax law in the HC treats it as ''transparent'' and non-taxable. The interest payable for the PC in the high tax country lowers the total profit. It is to keep in mind that all instalment payments and interest receivables remain in the holding. In this context, the TNC Holding abuses the different treatment of the different entities PC and S. Ultimately, this mismatch is exploited by a loan or bond. The TNC can shape its structure in a way that it can abuse different tax rates and interest or dividends deductibility conditions. According to Wachtel (2009) and Liebert (2004), this system also works with other expenditures such as labour costs.

The following case study, based on true events, illustrates this scenario. Going back to Figure 7 considers again a PC in the HC with high taxation and S with a hybrid entity in the FC with low taxation. Replacing the HC with countries, which play a leading role in fighting tax havens such as the USA or Germany (Wachtel, 2009), and the FC with the Cayman Islands, which have a high FS-Index pursuant to Table 1. The case ''Secret Letter Box''[4] is taken from the Focus (2007) by Elflein et al. It deals with an American software engineer who unofficially worked for O2 in Germany (HC). At the same time, being officially employed by a temp agency in the hybrid entity of O2 on the Channel Islands (FC) allowed his tax liabilities to reduce by around € 350,000. Then, the strategy of manipulating salaries in a hybrid entity also

---

[4] Originally, in German ''Geheimbriefkasten''.

paid off for O2 Germany which saved € 25 million in taxes. The strategy worked because O2 Germany sent a real, for those who worked in Germany (HC), and fake bill, for those who worked on the Channel Islands (FC), to the employees. The latter virtual pay check was around 50% higher which finally made the tax authorities, amongst others, suspicious. In the end, investigations caught O2 because of severe tax crimes and frauds. Apart from a tax economic view, this scandal proved also to be a social and moral one because O2 is reported to put pressure on its staff by revoking the working contract, for instance.

All in all, the hybrid entity mismatch with higher fake labour costs aims at reducing all costs arising from investment and employment. From an ethical point of view, it is unquestionably illegal and full of errors and bias. Therefore, any TNC taking this method as an underlying assumption for going abroad is unreliable and far away from economic and legal reality.

The final section summarizes and focuses on the problems from the three methods. Thereafter it moves from a problem oriented to a solution targeted approach giving each strategy a solution how to change the status quo.

III. Conclusion and possible solutions

After the introduction and evaluation of three exemplary methods of tax evasion, which include *founding subsidiaries abroad via real production shift, transfer pricing on paper* and *incurring debts and higher labour costs with hybrid entities on paper*, it has become clear that TNC's are taxed according to the local presence of their jurisdiction with the mayor business activities. In other words, they are treated as if they were loose collections of separate entities (S) operating in different countries (FC). The latter issues make use of the weak coordination and co-operation between tax authorities. Therefore, this ''separate (hybrid) entity'' approach gives TNC's scope to shift profits around the globe to suit their tax affairs.

Wachtel (2009) and Henn (2013) propose the *principle of a unitary taxation*. The PC in the HC with the entire S in the FC is considered as one unit/entity. More precisely, all profits are added and eventually divided by a measure index, taken from an apportionment formula. This measure index for the profits relies on features that cannot be shifted just on paper. It can be a combination of the annual turnover (sales), assets and the number of employees (wages). In conclusion, the principle of unitary taxation apportions the global profits of a TNC to the respective nations according to a weighted average formula. By so doing, the TNC holding publishes one combined financial report depicting the entire business activities. Therefore, each national tax authority detects the combined report and is finally capable of taxing the portion of the total profits at its own tax rate.

In my opinion, on the one hand, this principle works well in practice. It hinders transfer pricing with profit shifting and corresponds to the economic reality of a TNC. Both Wachtel (2009) and Henn (2013) agree that it has already become reality like in the U.S. state California where federal rules use the formula one third each feature implying assets, wages and sales. On the other hand, I do not think that it is efficient. It does not necessarily lead to more justice and transparency. In the EU, plans for a common consolidated corporate tax base are in the pipeline. However, the European Commission, Parliament and the Council have not yet found any agreement about the apportionment formula. It is still a voluntary multilateral application. It is hard to find such a formula because it may discriminate the poorer EU member states. Moreover, the EU law requires unanimity in tax issues. (Eimermann, 2005). Ultimately, I conclude that this principle simplifies the whole issue with a combined report, a clear definition of the business unit, tax base, and allocation formula with weighting factors. Hence, it is one solution to reduce global tax evasion due to transfer pricing and tax havens. It already works well in the U.S. but still is still in a complicated start position in the EU.

In contrast to treating the PC with all S as one entity, the *arm's length principle (ALP)* treats each PC with S as separate units. It requires any TNC to price the internal operations equal to external operations. For instance, PC sells a good at the same price from one S to another as if it was sold to a customer. Furthermore, the TNC has to set up different financial reporting accounts for each unit. On the one hand, it has already been applied because the

OECD and Germany, for example, endorsed it as an international standard and Foreign Tax Law. Subsequently, the national tax authority can start from the accounts of the TNC within the respective jurisdiction. On the other hand, this solution depends on a smooth country by country reporting mechanism where corporate transactions to governments are reported reliably. Hence, not every internal revenue service immediately detects the complicated tax accounts of the TNC as a whole. Murphy (2012) and Wachtel (2009) found out that TNCs may be reluctant to reveal their whole tax liabilities.

In conclusion, tax evasion undermines the authority of the national internal revenue services. It is possible by means of tax havens which offer a competitive advantage. They are the origins for tax crimes and frauds. The methods of a real production shift, transfer pricing on paper and incurring debts with associates with artificially high labour costs are symptoms of the ''disease''. By also counterfeiting the existence of tax havens, it is very likely that they loose their competitive advantage of monocultures in financial services including banking secrecy. Referring to the symptoms like transfer pricing, it is clear that tax dumping leads to price dumping for goods and services. Eventually, there is unfair and unfaithful competition. Therefore, in my eyes, tax evasion has to end. It is not an overnight procedure due to the complexity of the TNC's all over the world. Apart from a unitary taxation and the arm's length principle, one could also think of the advantages of a double taxation agreement, non deductibility with source taxation for future studies.

IV. Appendix

Table 1:

Financial Secrecy Index

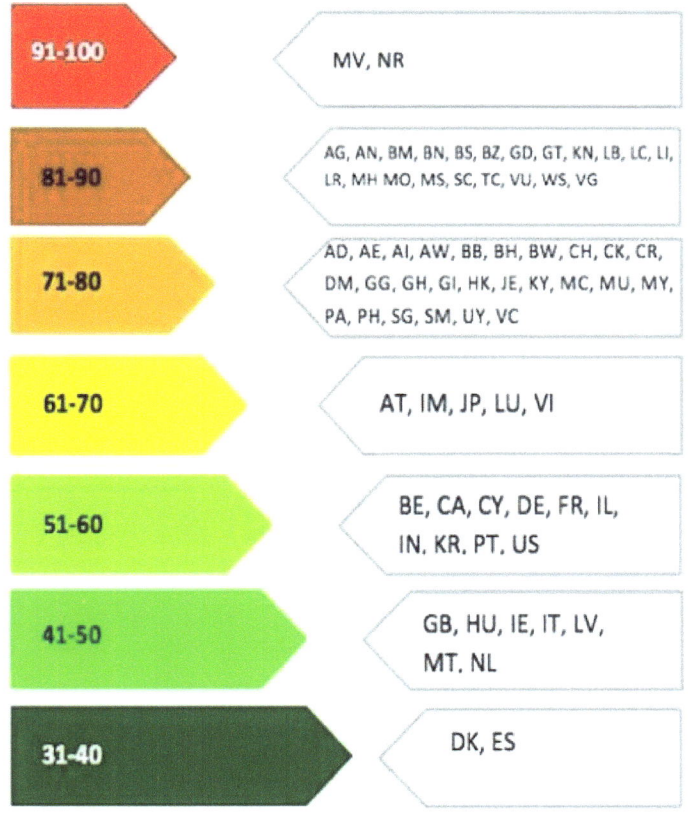

	Andorra (AD)		Korea (KR)
	Anguilla (AI)		Latvia (LV)
	Antigua & Barbuda (AG)		Lebanon (LB)
	Aruba (AW)		Liberia (LR)
	Austria (AT)		Liechtenstein (LI)
	Bahamas (BS)		Luxembourg (LU)
	Bahrain (BH)		Macau (MO)
	Barbados (BB)		Malaysia (Labuan) (MY)
	Belgium (BE)		Maldives (MV)
	Belize (BZ)		Malta (MT)
	Bermuda (BM)		Marshall Islands (MH)
	Botswana (BW)		Mauritius (MU)
	British Virgin Islands (VG)		Monaco (MC)
	Brunei Darussalam (BN)		Montserrat (MS)
	Canada (CA)		Nauru (NR)
	Cayman Islands (KY)		Netherlands (NL)
	Cook Islands (CK)		Netherlands Antilles (AN)
	Costa Rica (CR)		Panama (PA)
	Cyprus (CY)		Philippines (PH)
	Denmark (DK)		Portugal (Madeira) (PT)
	Dominica (DM)		Samoa (WS)
	France (FR)		San Marino (SM)
	Germany (DE)		Seychelles (SC)
	Ghana (GH)		Singapore (SG)
	Gibraltar (GI)		Spain (ES)
	Grenada (GD)		St Kitts & Nevis (KN)
	Guatemala (GT)		St Lucia (LC)
	Guernsey (GG)		St Vincent & Grenadines (VC)
	Hong Kong (HK)		Switzerland (CH)
	Hungary (HU)		Turks & Caicos Islands (TC)
	India (IN)		United Arab Emirates (Dubai) (AE)

	Ireland (IE)		United Kingdom (GB)
	Isle of Man (IM)		Uruguay (UY)
	Israel (IL)		US Virgin Islands (VI)
	Italy (IT)		USA (US)
	Japan (JP)		Vanuatu (VU)
	Jersey (JE)		

(Source: http://www.financialsecrecyindex.com/).

Figure 1:

Considering different tax rates

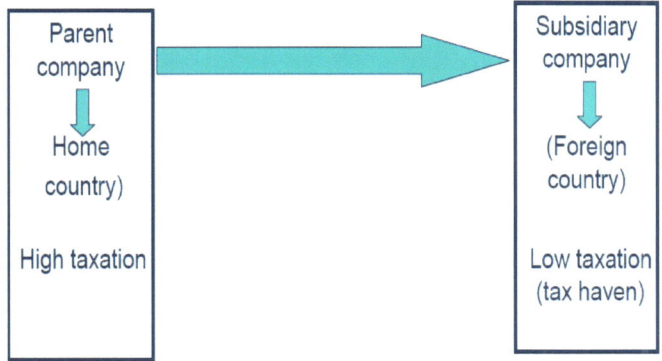

(Source: Own composition).

Figure 2:

Operative cycle

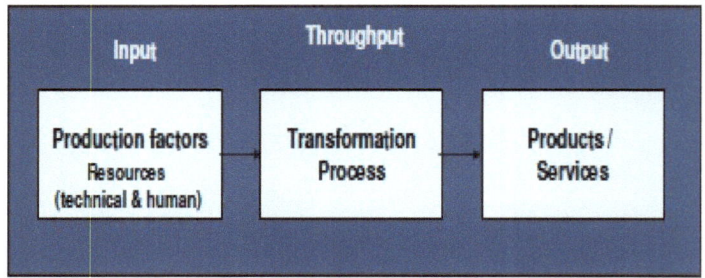

(Source: Own composition)

Figure 3:

Tax competition – Tax rates for corporate profits

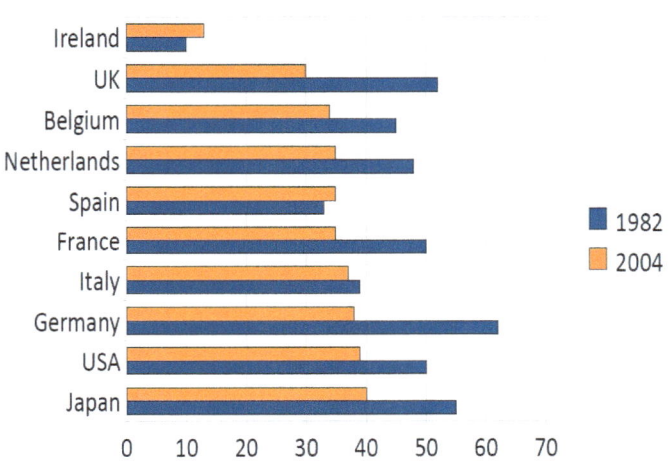

(Source: Henn, M., 2013, *Tax Havens and the Taxation of Transnational Corporations*. Berlin: WEED – World Economy, Ecology and Development.)

Table 2:

Determinants of FDI

Attribute	Hard Parameter	Soft Parameter
Labour	Labour Force	Knowledge
Transport Infrastructure	Transport Network	Efficiency
Major Participants	Original Equipment Manufacturer	Domestically and globally integrated value chain
Direct Internal Infrastructure	Related and supported industries Suppliers	Innovation Strategic partnerships Knowledge transfer
Indirect Internal Infrastructure	R&D institutions Universities	Knowledge Experience
Demand	Market size	Quality
State	Incentives	Cluster policy

(Source: Zschiedrich, H., 2006, *Ausländische Direktinvestitionen und regionale Industriecluster in Mittel- und Osteuropa.* Munich: Rainer Hampp Verlag.)

Figure 4:

A corporation – a nexus of contracts

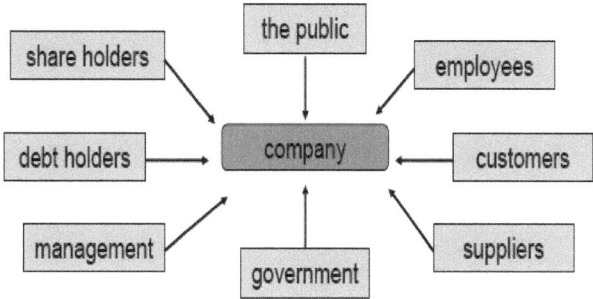

(Source: Own composition)

Figure 5:

Paper shift – Transfer pricing

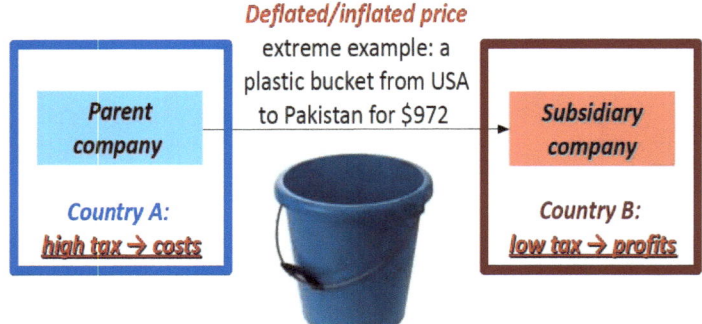

(Source: Henn, M., 2013, *Tax Havens and the Taxation of Transnational Corporations*. Berlin: WEED – World Economy, Ecology and Development.)

Figure 6:

''How to reduce the tax rate by 50%''

Step1:

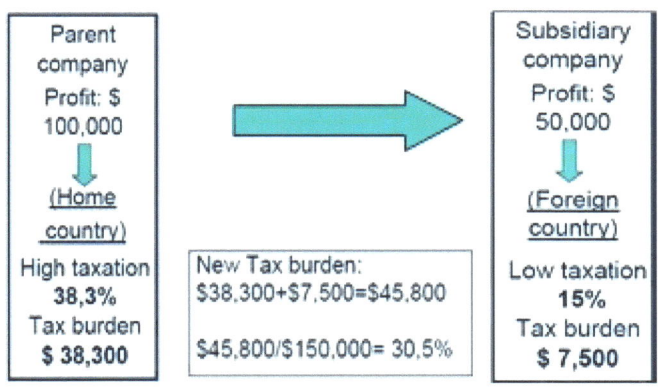

(Source: Own composition.)

Step 2:

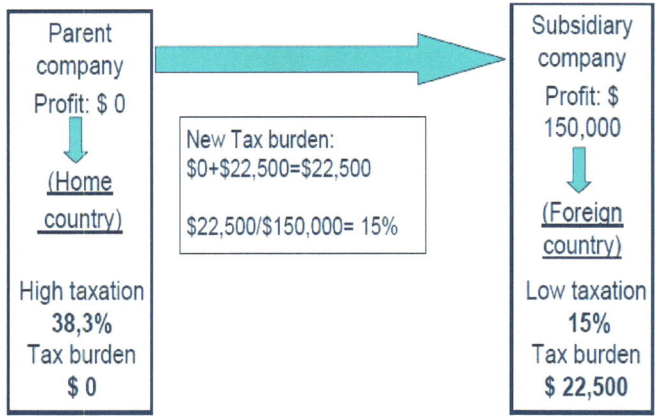

(Source: Own composition.)

Figure 7:

Paper shift: Hybrid entity mismatch

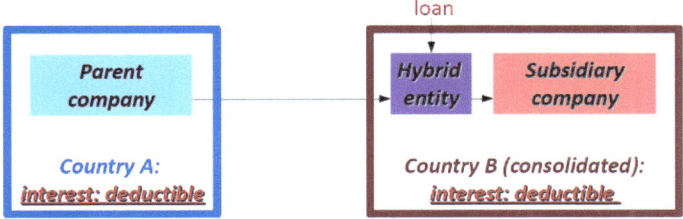

(Source: Henn, M., 2013, *Tax Havens and the Taxation of Transnational Corporations*. Berlin: WEED – World Economy, Ecology and Development.)

V. References

Buehn, A. and Schneider, F., 2012, Size and Development of Tax Evasion in 38 OECD Countries: What do we (not) know? [PDF] Available at http://www.cesifo-group.de/portal/pls/portal/ifo_applications.switches.DocLinkIfoDL?getDoc=cesifo1_wp4004.pdf [Accessed 26 May 2013].

Cloer, A. and Lavrelashvili, N., 2008, *Einführung in das Europäische Steuerrecht*. Berlin: Erich Schmidt Verlag GmbH & Co.

Eimermann, D., Giegold, S., Jarass, L., Kilmer, R., Kraus, A. and Liebert, N., 2005, *Globalisierung und Steuergerechtigkeit – Schritte gegen Steuerflucht und Steuerwettlauf nach unten*. Berlin: WEED – World Economy, Ecology and Development.

Focus 50, 2007, *Geheimbriefkasten 316*. [Online] Available at http://www.focus.de/finanzen/news/affaere-geheimbriefkasten-316_aid_229796.html [Accessed 26 May 2013].

Hebous, S., 2011, *Money at the Docks of Tax Havens*: A Guide. [PDF] Available at http://www.cesifogroup.de/portal/pls/portal/ifo_applications.switches.DocLinkIfoDL?getDoc=cesifo1_wp3587.pdf [Accessed 26 May 2013].

Heckmeyer, J. and Spengel, C., 2008, *Ausmaß der Gewinnverlagerung multinationaler Unternehmen –*

Empirische Evidenz und Implikationen für die deutsche Steuerpolitik. Berlin: WEED – World Economy, Ecology and Development.

Henn, M., 2013, *Tax Havens and the Taxation of Transnational Corporations*. Berlin: WEED – World Economy, Ecology and Development.

Klinter, S., Collins, C., Sklar, H., 2010, *Unfair Advantage: The Business Case against overseas tax havens*. Berlin: WEED – World Economy, Ecology and Development.

Liebert, N., 2004, *Globalisierung, Steuervermeidung und Steuersenkungswettlauf – Die zunehmende Umverteilung von unten nach oben*. Bonn: WEED – World Economy, Ecology and Development.

Murphy, R., 2012, *Country-by-Country Reporting. Accounting for globalisation locally.* [PDF] Available at http://www.taxresearch.org/uk/Documents/CBC2012.pdf [Accessed 26 May 2013].

Porter, M., 1998, *The Competitive Advantage of Nations. London*: McMillan.

Qari, S., 2012, *Tax avoidance, household information and inequality*. Berlin: Freie Universität.

Ruf, M., 2007, *Steuerwettbewerb in Europa – Theorie, Empirie und die Definition von Effektivsteuersätzen*. Wiesbaden: Deutscher Universitätsverlag.

Sandmo, A., 2005, *The theory of Tax Evasion: A retrospective view*. National Tax Journal 58(4): 643-663.

Social Watch Deutschland, 2007, *Würde und Menschenrechte wahren – Das Recht auf soziale Sicherheit für alle verwirklichen*. [PDF] Available at http://www.woek.de/web/cms/upload/pdf/social_watch/publikationen/swd_report_2007.pdf [Accessed 26 May 2013].

T-online, 2013, Steuer-Skandal: Uli Hoeneß stellt Strafanzeige wegen Enthüllung. [Online] Available at http://www.t-online.de/wirtschaft/id_63345314/uli-hoeness-stellt-strafanzeige-wegen-enthuellung-im-steuer-skandal-.html **[Accessed 26 May 2013].**

Wachtel, A., 2009, *Tax Havens in Europe - Their legal and economic implications*. Berlin: Hochschule für Wirtschaft und Recht.

Wahl, P., 2005, *International Taxation – Regulating Globalisation – Financing Development*. Berlin: WEED – World Economy, Ecology and Development.

Zschiedrich, H., 2006, *Ausländische Direktinvestitionen und regionale Industriecluster in Mittel- und Osteuropa*. Munich: Rainer Hampp Verlag.

www.ingramcontent.com/pod-product-compliance
Lightning Source LLC
Chambersburg PA
CBHW040339220526
45473CB00009B/2738